My First Spanish
Things Around Me at School

Picture Book with English Translations

Published By: MyFirstPictureBook.com

Mochila

Backpack

Campana

Bell

Libro

Book

Calculadora

Calculator

Calendario

Calendar

Cantina

Canteen

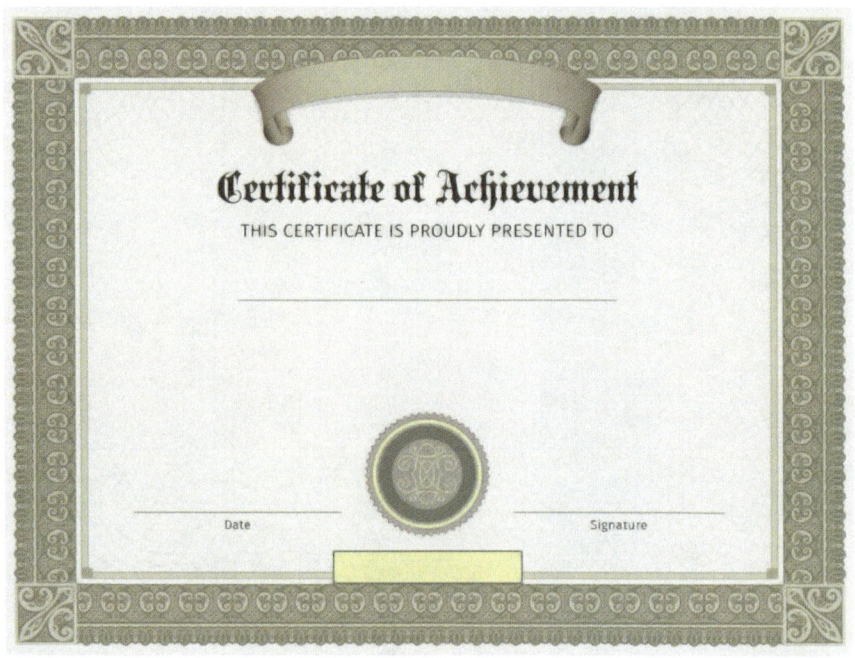

Certificado

Certificate

Silla

Chair

Tiza

Chalk

Pizarra

Chalkboard

Aula

Classroom

Ordenador

Computer

Escritorio

Desk

Goma de borrar

Eraser

Examen

Exam

Pegamento

Glue

Gimnasio

Gym

Biblioteca

Library

Mapa

Map

Papel

Paper

Lápiz

Pencil

Patio de recreo

Playground

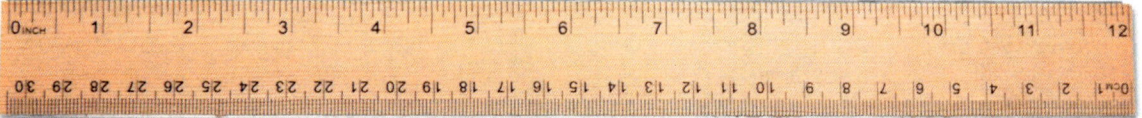

Regla

Ruler

Tentempié

Snack

Escalera

Stairs

Estudiante

Student

Mesa

Table

Cinta adhesiva

Tape

Profesora

Teacher

TIMETABLE

	Monday	Tuesday	Wednesday	Thursday	Friday
1					
2	History	Languages	Math	Biology	History
3	Math	Art	Economics	Chemistry	Art
4	Biology	Chemistry	Self-Defense	P.E	P.E
LD					
5	Chemistry	Biology	History	Technology	Languages
6	Economics	Technology	Languages	Math	Technology
AS	Self-Defense	Self-Defense	P.E	Art	Economics
C/C					

Horario

Timetable

30

Uniforme

Uniform

Pared

Wall

Made in United States
North Haven, CT
24 October 2022